T0413662

by Rebecca Phillips-Bartlett

Minneapolis, Minnesota

**Credits**
All images are courtesy of Shutterstock.com, unless otherwise specified. With thanks to Getty Images, Thinkstock Photo, and iStockphoto. Recurring – zhengzaishuru, K N, elyomys. Cover – Smileus. 4–5 – TTstudio, David Tadevosian. 6–7 – Dionisvera, Sergey Mironov, Lili.Q. 8–9 – Africa Studio, Gavran333, Yatra4289, Sabrina Janelle Gordon. 10–11 – Swapan Photography, Iurii Kachkovskyi, Anamaria Mejia, branex. 12–13 – elcatso, Pavlo Baliukh. 14–15 – Selina Irina, Maren Winter. 16–17 – Aleksandr Rybalko, Fotokostic, Vladimka production. 18–19 – Robert Kneschke, Michelle Sha. 20–21 – muratart, brulove, SOMMAI, Alexey Kabanov, su prasert, Pablesku. 22–23 – Davizro Photography, Somkid Saowaros.

**Bearport Publishing Company Product Development Team**
President: Jen Jenson; Director of Product Development: Spencer Brinker; Managing Editor: Allison Juda; Associate Editor: Naomi Reich; Associate Editor: Tiana Tran; Art Director: Colin O'Dea; Designer: Kim Jones; Designer: Kayla Eggert; Product Development Assistant: Owen Hamlin

Library of Congress Cataloging-in-Publication Data is available at www.loc.gov or upon request from the publisher.

ISBN: 979-8-88916-950-5 (hardcover)
ISBN: 979-8-88916-954-3 (paperback)
ISBN: 979-8-89232-127-3 (ebook)

© 2025 BookLife Publishing
This edition is published by arrangement with BookLife Publishing.

North American adaptations © 2025 Bearport Publishing Company. All rights reserved. No part of this publication may be reproduced in whole or in part, stored in any retrieval system, or transmitted in any form or by any means, electronic, mechanical, photocopying, recording, or otherwise, without written permission from the publisher. Bearport Publishing is a division of Chrysalis Education Group.

For more information, write to Bearport Publishing, 5357 Penn Avenue South, Minneapolis, MN 55419.

# CONTENTS

Plenty of Plants . . . . . . . . . . . . . . . 4
Cool Crops . . . . . . . . . . . . . . . . . . . 5
Grains. . . . . . . . . . . . . . . . . . . . . . . 6
Fruits and Vegetables . . . . . . . 8
Beyond Food . . . . . . . . . . . . . . . 9
Crafted Crops . . . . . . . . . . . . . .10
Crop Conditions. . . . . . . . . . . . .12
Growing Crops . . . . . . . . . . . . . .14
Growing Grains . . . . . . . . . . . . .16
Harvest Time . . . . . . . . . . . . . . .18
Identifying Crops . . . . . . . . . . . 20
Countless Crops. . . . . . . . . . . . 22
Glossary. . . . . . . . . . . . . . . . . . . 24
Index . . . . . . . . . . . . . . . . . . . . . 24

# PLENTY OF PLANTS

Our world is full of amazing plants. Many plants are found in the wild. Other plants are grown by humans.

Let's explore this *plant-iful* world all around us!

PLANTS CAN GROW IN THE GROUND, IN WATER, OR ON OTHER THINGS.

# COOL CROPS

Crops are plants that people grow to make things, such as food, clothing, and **medicine**. Farmers choose crops for their size, taste, or how well they sell as **products**.

CROPS ARE OFTEN GROWN IN LARGE FIELDS.

# GRAINS

Grains are some of the most common crops. They are the seeds from different types of grasses. Wheat, oat, rice, and corn are all types of grains.

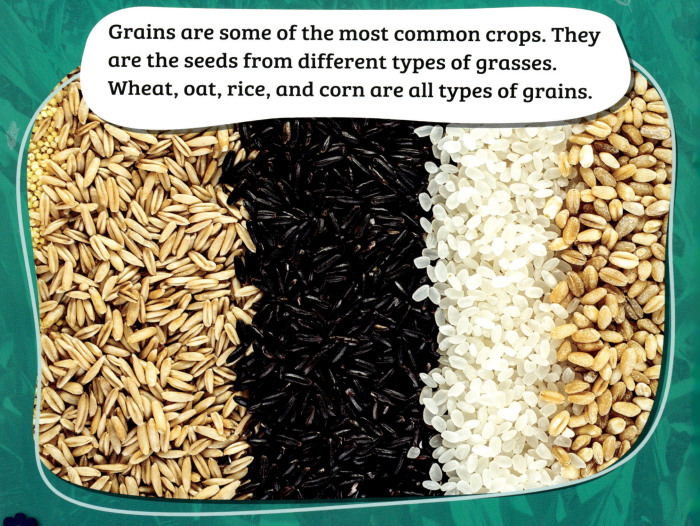

Grains are found near the tip of the plant. This part is called the ear.

Wheat seeds are often crushed into flour. This flour can be used to make breads, pastas, and cereals.

# FRUITS AND VEGETABLES

Fruits and vegetables are also grown as crops. Fruits are usually the sweet parts of plants that hold seeds. Veggies are other parts of plants that we eat, such as roots, leaves, and even flowers.

WE EAT THE LEAVES OF LETTUCE PLANTS.

# BEYOND FOOD

While lots of crops are grown to be eaten, some are made into other things. Some **materials**, such as cotton and rubber, are non-food crops. Cotton is often used to make clothing.

A cotton plant

Rubber comes from rubber trees.

# CRAFTED CROPS

Farmers carefully **breed** crops to get the best plants possible. They take seeds from plants that grew well in the past. That way, the new plants will be just as good!

THIS TYPE OF BREEDING HAS LED TO LARGER EARS OF CORN.

Sometimes, two types of a crop both have good **traits**. To get the best parts of both, farmers breed the plants together. This is called crossbreeding.

THE BANANAS WE EAT TODAY COME FROM CROSSBREEDING. ONE PLANT WAS SWEET BUT HAD LOTS OF SEEDS. THE OTHER PLANT WAS SEEDLESS BUT SOUR.

# CROP CONDITIONS

All plants need water and sunlight to grow. However, different plants need different amounts. Some farmers grow crops in **greenhouses** so they can better control their crops.

Farmers usually choose crops that will grow best in the weather where they live. Some plants, such as coffee and cocoa, grow better in warmer parts of the world. Carrots and kale grow better in cooler weather.

**COCOA IS A CROP USED TO MAKE CHOCOLATE.**

# GROWING CROPS

Growing the same crop in the same field again and again can harm the soil. To keep the soil healthy, some farmers switch the crops they grow in a field every year. This is called crop rotation.

Some fruits and nuts grow on trees. People grow these trees in orchards. Farmers often plant the trees in neat rows.

HAVE YOU EVER VISITED AN ORCHARD?

# GROWING GRAINS

Wheat is a very common grain. How is it grown?

First, the soil is dug up with a **plow**. Then, the seeds are planted in the soil.

16

The seeds need plenty of water and **nutrients**. A sprayer is often used to quickly give water and nutrients to whole fields of crops.

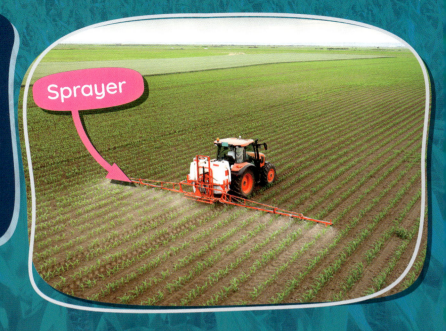

Sprayer

Once the wheat has grown, it is ready to be **harvested**. It's gathered with a large machine called a combine harvester.

Combine harvester

# HARVEST TIME

Most crops grow best at certain times of the year. Many grow during the warm summer months and are ready to be picked at the beginning of fall.

GRAPES AND PUMPKINS ARE CROPS THAT ARE OFTEN READY IN THE FALL.

There are many different ways to harvest crops. Grains are often collected with combine harvesters. But machines will smash softer crops, such as strawberries. These berries are usually picked by hand.

SOME PLANTS CAN MAKE YOU SICK. ALWAYS ASK A GROWN-UP BEFORE PICKING PLANTS.

# IDENTIFYING CROPS

Crops are used for all sorts of things! Can you match the descriptions below to the pictures on page 21?

1. Cotton is often used to make clothes. Its plants have brown stems. The cotton is white and fluffy.

2. Rice is one of the most popular foods in the world. It is a type of grain, which makes it a grass.

3. Sunflowers are large, yellow flowers. The seeds are often crushed to get their oil.

Answers: 1) Cotton is B. 2) Rice is C. 3) Sunflowers are A.

21

# COUNTLESS CROPS

From the food you eat to the clothes you wear, you come across crops every day. Think about the last thing you ate. Was it once growing in a field or on an orchard?

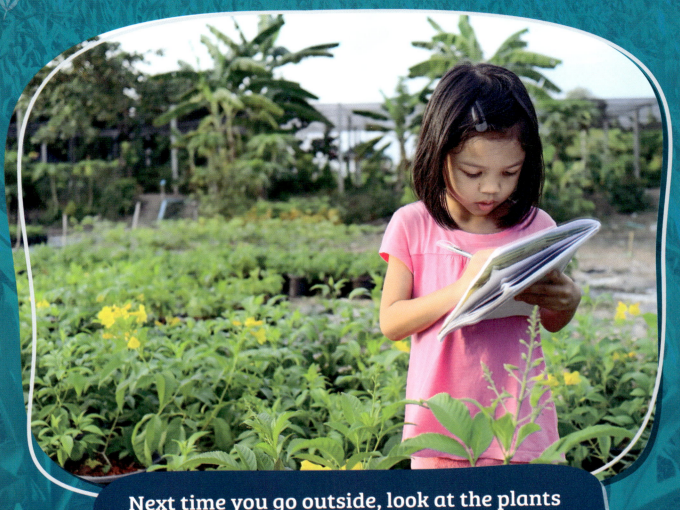

Next time you go outside, look at the plants near you. Could any of them be used to make something else? Write down what you see. There are plenty of plants to explore!

# GLOSSARY

**breed** to make more plants

**greenhouses** buildings, usually with glass roofs and walls, used for growing plants

**harvested** picked or gathered to be eaten

**materials** the elements that go into making something else

**medicine** something to fight off sickness or pain

**nutrients** substances that plants and animals need to grow and stay healthy

**plow** a tool used to dig up the ground

**products** things that are made and often offered for sale

**traits** qualities or characteristics of a living thing

# INDEX

**combine harvesters** 17, 19
**cotton** 9, 20–21
**crossbreeding** 11
**grains** 6–7, 10, 16, 19–20
**grapes** 18
**greenhouses** 12
**harvest** 17–19
**orchards** 15, 22
**trees** 9, 15
**wheat** 6–7, 16–17